LIFEWATCH

The Mystery of Nature

Egg to Snake

Oliver S. Owen

Published by Abdo & Daughters, 4940 Viking Drive, Suite 622, Edina, Minnesota 55435.

Library bound edition distributed by Rockbottom Books, Pentagon Tower, P.O. Box 36036, Minneapolis, Minnesota 55435.

Printed in the United States.

Cover Photo credit: Natural Selection
Interior Photo credits: Animals Animals

Edited By Bob Italia

LIBRARY OF CONGRESS CATALOGING-IN-PUBLICATION DATA

Owen, Oliver S., 1920—
    Egg to snake / Oliver S. Owen.
        p.   cm. -- (Life Watch)
    Includes Bibliographical references (p.) and Index (p.).
    ISBN 1-56239-294-8
    1. Snakes -- Juvenile literature. 2. Snakes-- Development -- Juvenile literature.
    [1. Snakes.] I. Title. II. Series: Owen, Oliver S., 1920 -   Lifewatch.
    QL666.06089 1994
    597.96--dc20   94-12943
                                                CIP
                                              AC

Contents

Snakes 4

Reproduction, Courtship and Mating.................... 9

Nests and Eggs..11

Hatching.. 14

The Young Snake 15

The Adult Snake.. 16

   Food and Feeding Behavior *16*

Defense Against Enemies...................................... 22

The Life Cycle 27

Glossary 28

Bibliography 30

Index.. 31

Snakes

When you hear or read the word "snake," what thoughts come to mind? That snakes are evil? That they are slimy? That they are poisonous? If so, you are wrong. Snakes are not evil at all. By feeding on crop-destroying rats and mice, they save farmers millions of dollars every year. Snakes are not slimy. If you rubbed your hand along their body, you would find them completely dry. And only a few snakes are poisonous. Most of them are harmless.

Scientists classify snakes as reptiles, along with lizards, crocodiles, alligators and turtles. All reptiles are coldblooded. This means that their body temperature changes with that of the environment. If a snake rests on a rock warmed by the sun, its body temperature will rise. If the rock cools off, the snake will get cooler, too. Like all reptiles, the snake's body is covered with hard parts of skin called scales.

A timber rattlesnake warming itself on a rock.

Snakes have a long, flexible, forked tongue. The snake does not sting with its tongue. The tongue is the snake's organ of touch. The snake constantly flicks the tongue out to "feel out" the ground over which it is about to move. This is especially helpful at night. Snakes do not have eyelids so they can't close their eyes. Because of this, scientists are not sure whether snakes sleep!

Notice the forked tongue on this garter snake.

Scientists recognize about 2,500 kinds of snakes in the world. However, only 110 species live in the United States. One in seven kinds of snakes are poisonous. Snakes are widely distributed. A few kinds are found as far north as the Arctic Circle. A large number live in the temperate regions. However, the largest population and variety of snakes occurs in the tropics of South America, Africa and Asia. New Zealand and Ireland lack snakes completely. Hawaii also had no snakes until humans brought over the flowerpot snake some years ago.

A South American anaconda, one of the largest snakes in the world.

The size of snakes varies greatly. The smallest are certain kinds of blind snakes, some of which are the size of earthworms. Most snakes in the United States range from two to five feet in length. The largest snake in North America is the eighteen-foot boa constrictor. A species of python in Asia gets to be 30 feet long. However, the world's largest snake is the giant anaconda of South America. Some of these snakes grow to be 37 feet long—about the length of six bicycles standing end to end!

Snakes do not live as long as humans. Most of the snakes crawling through the forests and grasslands of the United States probably live only five to fifteen years. The world record for "old age" among snakes belongs to a cobra which was kept in the San Diego Zoo. It lived to the ripe old age of 29 years!

Reproduction, Courtship and Mating

  Breeding activity in the warm tropics may occur at any time of the year. However, in the United States, the female's eggs and the male's sperm ripen during the winter, and the snakes breed in spring. How do the male and female snakes find each other? It is a problem. In some animals, like frogs and birds, the male's calls and songs attract the female. But snakes can't sing or call! So how do the two sexes get together?

These gray-banded king snakes are in the mating stage.

The female leaves a scent trail as she moves over the land. The male "picks up" the scent with the help of his tongue. He flicks it in and out while searching for the female. Once the male has found a female, he will start courting her. He crawls up to the female so that their bodies are side by side. Then he places his chin on her back and rubs it briskly. The male then moves forward while rubbing the female's back with his chin. This stimulates the female. The male then loops his tail around the tail of the female, and mating takes place. The male introduces sperm into the female's body and they fertilize her eggs.

This eastern garter snake is using its tongue to "sniff out" its mate.

Nests and Eggs

Most kinds of snakes reproduce by laying eggs. However, before the eggs are laid, the female will often make a simple nest. It may be just a shallow area which she has scraped out with her snout. Most snakes lay 10 to 15 eggs. The python of Asia, however, has been known to lay as many as a hundred! Many females will cover their eggs with soil or leaves so that egg-eating animals cannot find them. The soil also protects the eggs from the heat of the noon-day sun, or from the evening chill. This way, the egg temperature remains steady.

Snakes like to bury their eggs in the soil to protect them.

The rate at which the eggs hatch depends largely upon how warm they are. In birds, the warmth is provided by the mother bird's body while she "sits" on the eggs. The Indian python is one of the very few snakes which incubates its eggs like birds. However, a number of female cobras and pythons will build their nest in old piles of manure or garbage. This decaying material gives off a lot of heat. The yolk of a snake's egg has all the food which the embryo needs to develop into a baby snake. The embryo also needs water and oxygen which moves through the egg shell from the outside air.

This python is coiled around her brood of six eggs, incubating them.

A few snakes, like rattlesnakes and garter snakes, do not lay eggs. The females give birth to living young. The female rattlesnake may have up to 60 young at one time! In these live-bearing snakes, the egg develops inside the female's body. However, the egg shell is very thin and transparent. The embryo gets its water and oxygen from the mother's blood stream. The baby snakes hatch from the egg inside the mother's body and are born. Live-bearing has its advantages. Baby snakes that develop inside the mother's body are protected from egg-eating animals like foxes, skunks and raccoons. The embryo also develops in an environment where the temperature is more even than in an egg.

Hatching

The baby snake has a razor-sharp egg tooth on its upper jaw. It rubs this egg tooth back and forth on the inside of the egg shell. After some time, it cuts a hole in the shell. Then it pokes its tiny head through the hole. This egg-shell cutting is a lot of work. So the baby snake rests, sometimes for a whole day, with its head sticking out. Then it wriggles its way out of the egg and into a strange new world.

Newborn snakes struggle long and hard
to free themselves from their eggs.

The Young Snake

The newly born or hatched snakes get no protection or food from their parents. They are "on their own." Luckily, they are able to fend for themselves. They can find food and they can hide from enemies. Even though they are babies, some poisonous snakes can protect themselves when only a few days old. In fact, baby cobras have been known to strike at an enemy even though they are still only partly out of their egg!

Baby snakes are usually about one-fifth the length of their parents. During their first growing season, the young snakes may increase their length by 50 percent. Baby snakes living in the northern United States may go into hibernation (winter sleep) a few weeks after they hatch or are born. As the young snake grows, it will shed its skin from time to time. First, the snake rubs its snout against a rough surface. Gradually, the transparent outer skin will begin to peel away from the snout and jaws. Next, the snake will hook the front part of the old skin on a rock, log, or on the rough bark of a tree. Then it slowly crawls forward and out of its skin. The old skin is left behind and turned completely inside out. Snakes will shed their skins even when they are adults.

The Adult Snake

Food and Feeding Behavior

Snakes feed only on animals. Their prey range in size from tiny ants to full-grown deer! Many snakes are food specialists—they feed on only one kind of animal. One snake might feed only on ants. Some eat only termites. These snakes may live inside a termite nest so they are close to their food supply! The brown snake of the United States lives on a diet of earthworms. The meals of some tropical tree snakes are made up only of lizards. The American water snake feeds almost entirely on fish and frogs. Rabbits and squirrels are the main foods of the diamond-back rattlesnake of the United States. And some large snakes feed only on smaller snakes!

Snakes are able to eat animals that are three times the width of their head. This is possible because the bones of their jaws are not fastened tightly together. These bones can be spread apart as the snake eats a frog, rat, rabbit, or other animal it has just caught. Some large snakes, like the 30-foot reticulated python of southeast Asia, can swallow fully-grown deer that may weigh up to 140 pounds. (If you were a snake, you could easily swallow a quarter-pound hamburger, a fish, or

This photo shows a python swallowing a deer. The snake's jaw is detached, allowing it to open very wide.

even a whole roasted turkey without taking a single bite!) Your teeth are shaped for biting and chewing. Much of your chewing is done by the flattened molars at the back of your mouth. Snakes cannot chew their food because all their teeth end in a sharp needle-like point. The snake's teeth simply serve to seize the prey animal and force it into the throat.

Many snakes will eat only about every 10 days. After eating a wild pig or deer, a python may not eat again for two months.

Healthy snakes are able to live for a whole year without feeding. Most of the time snakes do not move around much. However, when a snake gets hungry, it might travel through meadows and woodlands for some distance in search of food. This is especially true of snakes that are active at night.

One summer day when the writer was camping in Minnesota, I was lucky enough to see a garter snake catch a frog. The snake crawled through the grass directly toward the frog. The frog did not see or hear the garter snake coming. When the snake got close enough, it suddenly lunged toward the frog and grabbed it with its jaws. Then it turned the frog around in its mouth and swallowed it head first. The sight of that frog kicking and squirming and finally disappearing down the snake's gullet will never be forgotten!

Snakes that are active in the day are often protectively colored. Their body matches the color of their background. Some tree snakes are bright green. They closely match the leaves over which they crawl. Other kinds of tree snakes are grayish-brown and blend in with tree bark. Woodland snakes are often colored brown or tan like the leaves of the forest floor. They simply lie in wait for a food animal, such as a mouse or rabbit, to walk or hop by. Then they lunge at the animal and seize it.

The color of this boa constrictor helps it blend in with its surroundings.

Small food animals, like ants and earthworms, can be eaten by a snake without any trouble. Larger animals may give snakes trouble. Toads will often gulp air and blow themselves up to prevent snakes from eating them. The hungry snake will then puncture the toad with its sharp teeth. The air escapes from the toad and its body shrinks so that the snake can swallow it.

A few snakes use lures to attract their prey. A good example is the copperhead of the United States. It has a tail which is colored a bright reddish-yellow. The rest of its body is rather dull in color. While waiting for prey, it will coil up with its tail hidden under its body. If a frog hops near the snake, the copperhead will raise its tail and wriggle it rapidly so that it looks like a big worm. The frog may try to eat the worm. But the frog soon winds up as a meal for the copperhead!

Some snakes have specialized methods for capturing and subduing their prey. One method is the injection of venom. The coral snakes and rattlesnakes of the United States, and the cobras of Asia and Africa use this method. The venom is injected with a pair of fangs which are located in the front of the upper jaw. These fangs are shaped something like a hypodermic (hi-poe-DER-mik) needle. A canal runs through each fang. Venom is secreted into the base of the fang and flows through the fang to the tip. When the snake strikes, the venom is injected into the body of the prey.

There are two main kinds of venoms. One kind destroys the red blood cells and causes severe bleeding. This is the venom found in poisonous snakes in the United States, such as the rattlesnake, copperhead, water moccasin and coral snake. The other kind affects the nerve and kills by paralyzing the breathing muscles and stopping the heartbeat. This is the kind found in cobras of Asia and Africa.

Another way in which snakes subdue their food animals is by constriction. The snake loops its muscular body around the prey to keep it from running away. Then it tightens its coils until the prey dies from suffocation. The bull snake and king snake of the United States use this method to kill the rats and mice on which they feed. The boa constrictors of North America and the pythons of Asia and Africa also are constrictors.

A sixteen-foot rock python from Africa used constriction to kill an impala (antelope) that weighed at least 130 pounds! There are many stories of huge pythons killing and eating humans. However, there is only one official record of such a tragedy. Some years ago, a reticulated python caught, killed and swallowed a 14-year-old boy on a southeast Asian island.

The fangs of a diamondback snake.
Notice the dripping venom.

Defense Against Enemies

In the United States, snakes are often eaten by skunks, opossum and wild pigs. Many kinds of hawks will feed on snakes. They will soar on motionless wings as they look down for snakes crawling through a grassy field. Several times, the writer has seen a red-tailed hawk seize a snake in its talons and fly away with its squirming meal. Wild turkeys will even attack rattlesnakes. In Africa, the mongoose and secretary bird are noted for their snake-killing behavior. Surprisingly, other snakes, such as the racers and coral snakes of the United States and the cobras of Asia and Africa, are the greatest enemies.

How do snakes protect themselves from all these would-be snake-eaters? You might think that they could simply crawl away. Most snakes, however, are pretty slow—crawling at a top speed of about 2-3 miles per hour (you can walk faster than that). A few snakes, like the American racers, can flee from their enemies at a speed of seven miles an hour. Some snakes simply avoid their enemies by burrowing into the ground or by hiding under rocks and logs. Many snakes escape notice by "freezing" when an enemy gets close.

Many snakes are protectively colored—matching the soil, rocks, branches and leaves over which they crawl. Desert snakes are often colored like the sand in which they live. Some snakes have patches of color or dark lines which "break their body into pieces." A snake-eating animal might look right at such a snake without recognizing it. Certain desert snakes have special spines on the snout which stick out. An enemy might run past such a snake partly covered with sand and miss a good meal.

This cobra is flaring its neck out, ready to strike.

Notice the rattle on the tail of this rattlesnake. The snake sounds it to scare off enemies.

Some African vipers raise and bend the front part of their body when an enemy gets close. The viper then looks like a broken branch and escapes being eaten.

Many snakes have special behaviors which surprise or threaten their enemies. Some will take in air so that they suddenly look bigger. Others will rise up and change the shape of their necks to startle their enemies. The neck of the South American chicken snake becomes egg-shaped. The cobra flattens its neck into a "warning hood." The coral snakes of southern United States have bright bands of red, black and yellow. This warning coloration advertises the dangerous nature of these snakes to enemies which might think of eating them.

The American king snake closely mimics the color pattern of the coral snake. Some scientists believe it gets some protection in this way.

Some snakes make special sounds which threaten their enemies. The American rattlesnakes shake the "rattles" in their tails and make buzzing sounds. Snakes have no voice. But many will make loud hissing sounds by forcing air from their lungs. This has a protective function. When an enemy gets close, the American hook-nosed snake makes loud popping sounds by forcing air through its vent. The strange noise frightens would-be snake-eaters.

This diamondback rattlesnake is in striking position.

One of the most amazing threat displays is that of the American hog-nosed snake. This small, harmless snake has a snout which is turned up like that of a hog. When an enemy, such as a skunk, gets too close, it blows itself up and starts hissing loudly. Then it suddenly turns over on its back, jerks a few times, and lies still with its tongue hanging out. It is playing "dead"! This is a good way to defend itself against animals that feed only on living snakes.

The hog-nosed snake pretends that it is dead when defending itself against enemies.

The cobra defends itself by "spitting" venom at its attacker. It forces the venom through its two fangs by squeezing the poison glands on the sides of its mouth. The cobra can "spit" the poison five feet. It directs the poison into the eyes of its enemy, causing damage and great pain.

The Life Cycle

Most of their adult lives, snakes either search for food or try their best to avoid getting eaten by other animals. If they are successful, they will have a chance to reproduce. Many snakes, such as the American garter snake, will breed by the time they are three or four years old.

We have followed the life of snakes from the egg to baby snake to adult and back to the egg again. It's an amazing story, don't you think?

GLOSSARY

Constriction   A snake's method of killing an enemy by throwing loops about their body and then tightening them to cause suffocation.

Egg tooth   A sharply-pointed tooth which is used by the baby snake to cut its way out of the egg.

Embryo   The young snake which is developing inside the egg.

Fang   The tooth in the upper jaw of a poisonous snake which injects poison into the prey.

Hibernation   A type of "winter sleep."

Live-bearer   A snake which gives birth to its young.

Protective

Coloration   A type of coloration which makes the snake match its background and protects it from its enemies.

Scales   Hardened pieces of skin which cover the snake's body.

Venom   Secretion made by the poison gland of the snake.

Vent   The opening at the base of a snake's tail through which the wastes pass from the body.

Warning

Coloration   The bright color of a poisonous snake which advertises its dangerous nature to its enemies.

Bibliography

Barker, Will. *Familiar Reptiles and Amphibians of North
America.* New York: Harper and Row, 1964.

Encyclopedia Americana. "Snakes" entry. Danbury, Conn.:
Grolier, 1994.

Leviton, Alan. *Reptiles and Amphibians of North America.* New
York: Doubleday and Company, Inc., 1971.

Parker, H. W. *Snakes: A Natural History.* (2nd ed.) Ithaca,
N.Y.: Cornell University Press, 1977.

World Book Encyclopedia. "Snakes" entry. Chicago: Field
Enterprises, 1990.

Index

A

Africa 7, 20, 21, 22, 24
alligator 4
anaconda 8
ant 6, 16, 19
Arctic Circle 7
Asia 7, 8, 11, 16, 20, 21, 22

B

baby snakes 13
blind snake 8
boa constrictor 8, 20
body temperature 4
breeding 9

C

cobra 8, 12, 15, 20, 22,
    24, 27
coldblooded 4
copperhead 19, 20
coral snakes 20, 22, 24
crocodile 4

D

deer 16, 17
desert snakes 23

E

earthworms 8, 16, 19
egg tooth 14
eggs 9, 10, 11, 12, 13
embryo 12, 13
enemies 15, 22, 24, 25

F

fangs 20, 27
feeding 4, 18
fish 16
flowerpot snake 7
forked tongue 6
foxes 13
frog 9, 16, 18, 19

G

garter snake 13, 18, 27
grasslands 8

H

hatched snakes 15
hibernation 15
hog-nosed snake 26
humans 7, 8, 21

M

mating 9,10
meadows 18
mice 4, 20

N

nest 11, 12, 16
New Zealand 7

P

poison 4, 7, 15, 20, 27
prey 16, 17, 19, 20
python 8, 11, 12, 16, 17,
    18, 20, 21

R

rats 4, 20
rattlesnake 13, 16, 20,
    22, 25
reptile 4

S

San Diego Zoo 8
scales 4
scent 10
shed 15
skin 4, 15
skunks 13, 22
snake-eaters 22, 25
snout 11, 15, 23, 26
South America 7, 8, 24
sperm 9, 10
spines 23

T

temperate region 7
termites 16
toads 19
tropics 7, 9
turtle 4

V

venom 20, 27
vipers 24

W

water moccasin 20
woodlands 18

About the Author

Oliver S. Owen is a Professor Emeritus for the University of Wisconsin at Eau Claire. He is the coauthor of *Natural Resource Conservation: An Ecological Approach* (Macmillan, 1991). Dr. Owen has also authored *Eco-Solutions* and *Intro to Your Environment* (Abdo & Daughters, 1993). Dr. Owen has a Ph.D. in zoology from Cornell University.

To my grandson, Amati,
may you grow up to always
appreciate and love nature.
— Grandpa Ollie